Minooka Community High School
District 111
Channahon, IL 60410

The Vampire Library

Vampires
in Literature

KRIS HIRSCHMANN

ReferencePoint Press®

San Diego, CA

About the Author

Kris Hirschmann has written more than 200 books for children. She owns and runs a business that provides a variety of writing and editorial services. She lives just outside Orlando, Florida, with her husband, Michael, and her daughters, Nikki and Erika.

©2011 ReferencePoint Press, Inc.

For more information, contact:
ReferencePoint Press, Inc.
PO Box 27779
San Diego, CA 92198
www.ReferencePointPress.com

Picture credits:
Cover: Dreamstime
Fortean Picture Library: 19
iStockphoto.com: 5, 10, 17
Landov: 36, 49, 59
Photofest: 24, 26, 31, 47, 67, 70

Series design and book layout:
Amy Stirnkorb

LIBRARY OF CONGRESS CATALOGING-IN-PUBLICATION DATA

Hirschmann, Kris, 1967-
  Vampires in literature / by Kris Hirschmann.
     p. cm. -- (Vampire library)
  Includes bibliographical references and index.
  ISBN-13: 978-1-60152-134-7 (alk. paper)
  ISBN-10: 1-60152-134-0 (alk. paper)
  1. Vampires in literature. I. Title.
  PN56.V3H57 2011
  809'.93375--dc22

                                              2010010104

Contents

Immortal Attraction

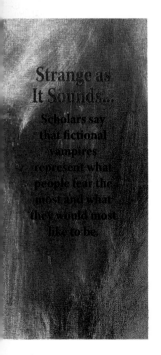

The 1897 novel *Dracula* contains some of the spookiest images in literary history. One of them is the moment Jonathan Harker, a lawyer who is being held prisoner in Count Dracula's castle, decides to search the count's coffin for a key. Harker raises the coffin's lid, and then he says:

> I saw something which filled my very soul with horror. There lay the Count, but looking as if his youth had been half restored. For the white hair and moustache were changed to dark iron-grey. The cheeks were fuller, and the white skin seemed ruby-red underneath. The mouth was redder than ever, for on the lips were gouts of fresh blood, which trickled from the corners of the mouth and ran down over the chin and neck. Even the deep, burning eyes seemed set amongst swollen flesh, for the lids and pouches underneath were bloated. It seemed as if the whole awful creature were simply gorged with blood. He lay like a filthy leech, exhausted with his repletion.[1]

Bram Stoker's Dracula, *published in 1897, became a classic of vampire literature. In one memorable scene, young hero Jonathan Harker opens a coffin in search of a key but instead finds Count Dracula, his flesh swollen and blood trickling from his mouth.*

This gruesome passage is a classic portrait of the vampire, a supernatural being that is part human, part monster, and all horrible. With their origins in ancient legend, these bloodsucking creatures of the night have haunted humankind's nightmares for thousands of years. About two centuries ago they started popping up in works of literature. They have been a staple of fiction ever since. It seems that vampires have an irresistible hold on the reading public's imagination.

The Scare Factor

The scare factor is one reason for this fascination. Dracula and many of his fictional kin seem to ooze evil. They stalk, feed, and kill without mercy, using their otherworldly powers to subdue and seduce their human prey. As if this were not bad enough, a vampire's victims sometimes turn into vampires themselves. It is a terrifying idea: To be hunted, and fed upon, and to die—and then to become a monster oneself. This scenario has provided chills and thrills for generations of readers.

Some people find this type of fare disturbing. They would never crack open a horror book. But many of these readers are just fine with the kinder, gentler vampires that populate today's bookshelves. Imaginative writers have squeezed vampires into every possible literary genre, including romance, comedy, science fiction, teen and children's literature, and much more. The result is that readers of every taste and age are now getting sucked into vampire books.

This interest has had a huge impact on the publishing and bookselling industries. Today bookstores stock entire aisles with vampire literature, both classic and modern. Publishing houses churn out new titles and series to meet this demand. The result has been a virtual bloodbath of vampire books. In early 2010 one Web site listed nearly 5,000 works of vampire fiction for sale.

This may seem like overkill. But to vampire fans there appears to be no such thing as too much. Readers continue to buy books about vampires, and they seem to be endlessly fascinated by them. The field of vampire literature will undoubtedly continue to thrive as long as this fascination endures.

Chapter 1

Laying the Foundation

Vampire myths and legends have been around for thousands of years. They appear in the writings of the ancient Greeks, in Aztec carvings, and in the spoken stories of India and the Far East. Tales of the undead were especially important in eastern Europe. In this region, vampires were once considered an unpleasant but very real fact of daily life.

Early vampire writings were retellings. They were meant to record old stories, not create original ones. But a couple of centuries ago, an important change took place. Writers started to reimagine vampires as fictional characters with vivid personalities, traits, and powers. In doing so, they created an all-new view of the vampire existence.

Vampire fiction hit an immediate vein of popularity. It also established conventions for the way vampires should look and act. It laid the groundwork for the vast body of vampire literature that would eventually follow.

First Blood

The first known work of vampire fiction hit the shelves in 1819. Called *The Vampyre: A Tale*, this short story was written by a physician named John Polidori. It was based on a story that had been told by the famous poet Lord Byron, who was

Polidori's friend and travel companion.

In *The Vampyre*, a handsome but evil nobleman named Lord Ruthven befriends a younger man named Aubrey. Aubrey is fascinated by Ruthven at first. As time goes by, though, he sees that Ruthven has bad effects on the people around him. One by one, Ruthven's friends fall into ruin and disgrace. Some even die. Aubrey starts to suspect that Ruthven is evil. Or even worse—he might just be a vampire.

One night a band of thieves gives Ruthven a fatal wound. In his final throes, Ruthven makes Aubrey promise to tell no one of his death. Aubrey agrees. Imagine Aubrey's surprise when Ruthven reappears a few weeks later and begins to woo Aubrey's younger sister! Almost sure now that Ruthven is a vampire, but bound by his promise, Aubrey watches in horror as the relationship progresses. Ruthven eventually marries Aubrey's sister, who becomes a meal for the bloodsucker on her wedding night.

The Vampyre is a very simple story. With its humanlike vampire, however, the tale broke new ground. It introduced the notion that vampires could walk among people and even fit in to their social circles. In Polidori's world, anyone—a casual acquaintance, a best friend, or even a fiancé—could potentially be a bloodsucking monster. This is a complete turnaround from Slavic legends, which usually described vampires as filthy, gibbering, animalistic creatures.

It is also important that Ruthven does not appear to be just *any* human. He is an aristocratic, handsome, appealing human. In fact, he is supernaturally appealing. Polidori uses these words to describe Ruthven's effect on others:

> His peculiarities caused him to be invited to every house; all wished to see him, and those

Strange as It Sounds...

The Vampyre was originally published under Lord Byron's name. Polidori eventually received full credit after Byron denied writing the story.

who had been accustomed to violent excitement, and now felt the weight of ennui [boredom], were pleased at having something in their presence capable of engaging their attention. In spite of the deadly hue of his face, which never gained a warmer tint . . . though its form and outline were beautiful, many of the female hunters after notoriety attempted to win his attentions.[2]

Ruthven's attractiveness makes him, in a way, even more horrible. It means that he is the ultimate predator. He does not chase his prey; he simply tricks people into coming too close. Anyone, no matter how well-meaning or careful, could become the vampire's next victim.

Plenty Dreadful

Polidori's ideas were expanded to gruesome effect in the next major work of vampire literature. *Varney the Vampire, or the Feast of Blood*, by Thomas Preskett Prest, was published in weekly installments from 1845 to 1847. The story line involves the vampire Sir Francis Varney and the troubles he visits upon the unfortunate Bannerworth family, who appear to be Varney's direct descendents.

Works in serial form, including *Varney the Vampire*, were once known as "penny dreadfuls." *Varney* certainly earned this nickname. Prest's writing drips with overblown adjectives and lurid descriptions. The characters' dialogue (of which there is a great deal) is full of exclamations and melodrama. And the story has more twists and turns than a modern-day soap opera. It is over-the-top fun—and readers loved every word. *Varney* was incredibly successful, eventually stretching

Strange as It Sounds...
Suave, sophisticated vampires who walk among humans are known in literary circles as drawing-room vampires. Such a vampire is at home anywhere—even, as the term suggests, in an upper-class drawing room where visitors are greeted and entertained.

The lurid descriptions and soap opera–like twists of Varney the Vampire, or the Feast of Blood, *captivated readers in the mid-1800s. Shown here is an illustration from one of the story's weekly installments.*

to 220 chapters and covering 860 pages of text.

Much of *Varney*'s appeal was due to its horrible yet fascinating main character. Like Lord Ruthven, Varney is an aristocrat. Unlike Ruthven, however, Varney is truly monstrous. When he is well fed, he can pass as a human. But he changes into a frightful creature when his vampire nature emerges. In the series' first installment, Prest vividly describes one such incident:

> The figure turns half round, and the light falls upon the face. It is perfectly white—perfectly

bloodless. The eyes look like polished tin; the lips are drawn back, and the principal feature next to those dreadful eyes is the teeth—the fearful looking teeth—projecting like those of some wild animal, hideously, glaringly white, and fang-like. It approaches the bed with a strange, gliding movement. It clashes together the long nails that literally appear to hang from the finger ends.[3]

Varney's terrifying transformations brought an element of vampire legend back onto the scene. They also introduced the idea that vampires could change their looks or form. This concept was destined to become part of vampire lore. It would be adapted by many authors in the centuries to follow.

So would the idea of vampire hypnotism. Varney was the first vampire who could mesmerize his victims, making it impossible for them to escape his deadly kiss. As Prest writes: "The glance of a serpent could not have produced a greater effect upon her than did the fixed gaze of those awful, metallic-looking eyes. . . . She cannot withdraw her eyes from that marble-looking face. He holds her with his glittering eye."[4]

Supernatural healing powers were yet another concept that arose in the Varney series. Although Varney can be wounded, moonlight heals him almost instantly. This fact causes endless headaches for Varney's human opponents. The Bannerworth clan nearly kills their vampire foe countless times, only to be thwarted when Varney flees under the light of the full moon.

Varney may have been hard to kill. He was not, however, immortal. In the series' final installment, Varney commits suicide by flinging himself into the mouth of a lava-filled volcano. It is a fittingly dramatic death for one of vampire literature's most dramatic characters.

The Original Vampire

Drama was also on tap in a novella called *Carmilla*. This time, though, the action had a feminine twist. Written in 1872 by J. Sheridan Le Fanu, *Carmilla* was the first work to feature a female vampire.

Carmilla is narrated by a character named Laura, a young woman who lives with her widowed father in a fictitious European realm called Styria. Laura's simple life takes a sinister turn when a dark carriage overturns in front of her home. The carriage contains two people: Carmilla, a girl about Laura's age who seems to be injured, and Carmilla's mysterious mother. The mother quickly leaves on what she terms "urgent business," leaving Carmilla in the care of Laura and her father.

Laura and Carmilla soon become close friends. But Laura notices some strange things about her new companion. Carmilla will not share any personal information. She rests most of the day and sleepwalks at night. She also has a disturbing reaction one day when Laura sings a Christian hymn:

> Her face underwent a change that alarmed and even terrified me for a moment. It darkened, and became horribly livid; her teeth and hands were clenched, and she frowned and compressed her lips, while she stared down upon the ground at her feet, and trembled all over with a continued shudder as irrepressible as ague [feverish shivering]. All her energies seemed strained to suppress a fit.[5]

A Gruesome Game

The idea for *The Vampyre* was born during a famous game. In May 1816 John Polidori was traveling with Lord Byron, who was quite well known at the time. The pair met up in Switzerland with poet Percy Shelley and his 18-year-old wife-to-be, Mary Wollstonecraft Godwin.

One stormy night the foursome decided to entertain themselves by telling ghost stories. Polidori invented a yarn about a "skull-headed lady." Lord Byron, when his turn came, told a tale about a traveling vampire and his unfortunate human companion. This story later became the basis for Polidori's *The Vampyre*.

The Vampyre was not the only significant story to come out of the historic contest. Young Mary Godwin, too, produced an idea that had a lasting effect on the literary world. Godwin spun a tale about a reanimated corpse that longs for love and acceptance. She later expanded her story and published it under her married name, Mary Shelley. The work's title was *Frankenstein*, and it went on to become one of the most famous horror novels of all time.

Most worrisome of all, Laura starts to have recurring nightmares. She dreams that she is being stalked and bitten in the chest by a black cat, which sometimes turns into a human female afterward. As the dreams continue, Laura's health declines rapidly.

Concerned, Laura's father turns to his friends for advice. He discovers that one of his acquaintances had a similar experience when a woman named Millarca stayed with his family. The friend's daughter, unfortunately, did not survive the visit.

After this revelation, Laura's father is even more worried. He does more research. He eventually discovers that both Carmilla and Millarca are really the Countess Mircalla Karnstein, a supposedly dead relative. The vampire countess is hunted and destroyed, never to trouble Laura or any other young woman again.

Creepy and Original

Scholars consider *Carmilla* important for two main reasons. First, this tale introduced several conventions that would appear in later vampire stories. Carmilla occasionally sleeps in a coffin. She can change into an animal (in this case, a black cat). And she seems to feel physical discomfort when confronted by religious symbols and activities. These ideas are familiar to modern readers. But in Le Fanu's time, they were creepy and original.

Even more original was the character of Carmilla herself. Not only was Carmilla the first female vampire, she was also the first *lesbian* vampire. Le Fanu's language skirted the subject a bit, as was considered proper for the times. But passages like this one leave little doubt about Le Fanu's intentions:

Strange as It Sounds...

Dracula is an epistolary novel. This means that the story is told as a series of documents (letters, diary entries, newspaper clippings, and so on).

My strange and beautiful companion would take my hand and hold it with a fond pressure, renewed again and again; blushing softly, gazing in my face with languid and burning eyes, and breathing so fast that her dress rose and fell with the tumultuous respiration. It was like the ardour of a lover; it embarrassed me; it was hateful and yet overpowering; and with gloating eyes she drew me to her, and her hot lips travelled along my cheek in kisses; and she would whisper, almost in sobs, "You are mine, you shall be mine, and you and I are one for ever."[6]

The lesbian vampire hit a chord with readers. The idea was both scary and steamy, which made it the perfect recipe for chills and thrills. Carmilla was destined to become an archetype, or model, for many future literary vampires.

Bram Stoker's *Dracula*

When it comes to archetypes, of course, one fictional vampire stands head and fangs above all the rest. The fiend's name is—what else?—Count Dracula.

Count Dracula was the brainchild of Bram Stoker, an Irish author with a background in theater. *Dracula* was published in 1897, when Stoker was 50 years old. Today the novel has been re-created so many times, in so many forms, that its plot is familiar to most people. But it is such a literary milestone that it bears retelling—if only for its delicious fright factor.

Dracula opens during the travels of Jonathan Harker, an English lawyer. Harker has been summoned to Transylvania

Strange as It Sounds...

In Vlad Dracula's name, the word *dracula* means "son of the dragon."

to help the mysterious Count Dracula with a real estate transaction. He takes a hair-raising coach ride to Dracula's crumbling castle. There he is greeted by the creepy count, who is described in this passage:

> His face was a strong, a very strong, aquiline, with high bridge of the thin nose and peculiarly arched nostrils, with lofty domed forehead, and hair growing scantily round the temples but profusely elsewhere. His eyebrows were very massive, almost meeting over the nose, and with bushy hair that seemed to curl in its own profusion. The mouth, so far as I could see it under the heavy moustache, was fixed and rather cruel-looking, with peculiarly sharp white teeth. These protruded over the lips, whose remarkable ruddiness showed astonishing vitality in a man of his years. For the rest, his ears were pale, and at the tops extremely pointed. The chin was broad and strong, and the cheeks firm though thin. The general effect was one of extraordinary pallor.
>
> Hitherto I had noticed the backs of his hands as they lay on his knees in the firelight, and they had seemed rather white and fine. But seeing them now close to me, I could not but notice that they were rather coarse, broad, with squat fingers. Strange to say, there were hairs in the centre of the palm. The nails were long and fine, and cut to a sharp point.[7]

Despite his host's odd appearance, Harker finds his stay pleasant enough at first. Soon, though, Harker realizes that he is being held prisoner in Dracula's castle. He starts to experience ever-more-disturbing things. He notices, for instance, that he cannot see his host's reflection in a mirror. He spots Dracula crawling up the castle's wall like a fly. And one night, roaming the castle against Dracula's strict orders, he is attacked by three female fiends. He is saved in the nick of time by Dracula, who still needs Harker's help to complete his land purchase.

Harker eventually escapes Dracula's castle and returns to England. Shortly thereafter, a ship runs aground near Harker's hometown. All of the crew are missing and presumed dead. The ship's log, however, is still aboard. It describes a series of strange and apparently supernatural events that led to the crew's demise. It also lists the ship's cargo: boxes containing "mould," or soil, from Transylvania.

Varney escaped death on many occasions but his escapades finally came to a dramatic conclusion when he jumped into the mouth of a lava-filled volcano—ending his life as well as the stories that had entertained readers for about two years.

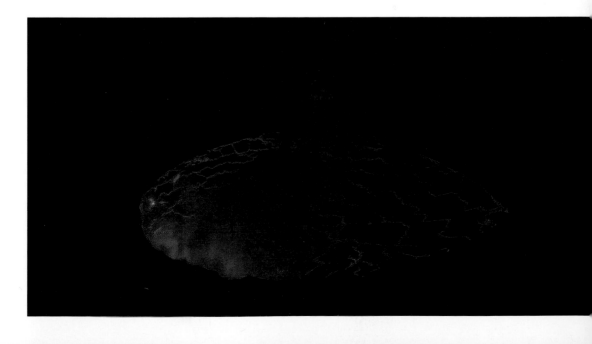

Odd Occurrences

Before long, odd things start to happen. Lucy Westenra, a friend of Harker's bride, Mina, dies after wasting away for no apparent reason. A professor named Abraham Van Helsing determines that Lucy has been the victim of a vampire, and as such, is now a vampire herself. He leads three men (all of whom had been Lucy's suitors) to Lucy's tomb. The men find Lucy roaming the graveyard as a vampire, fresh blood streaming from her mouth. Lucy's fiancé kills his former love by driving a stake through her heart.

Furious, Dracula next turns his attention to Mina. He bites her three times and feeds her his own blood. As Mina's health declines, it becomes clear that she has formed a psychic bond with the vampire. Van Helsing cleverly uses this bond to track Dracula's movements. He discovers that Dracula is fleeing back to Transylvania.

Van Helsing and his band of vampire hunters follow Dracula. They catch up to the count's carriage near Castle Dracula just before sunset. They throw open Dracula's coffin and find the helpless vampire inside. They slit Dracula's throat and stab him through the heart. The vampire crumbles into dust, forever freeing Mina—and the rest of the world—from his terrible presence.

Makings of a Classic

Although *Dracula* got good reviews when it was first published, it was not an immediate best seller. As the decades went by, however, Stoker's novel became more and more popular. Today *Dracula* is considered a classic. It has been reprinted hundreds of times in dozens of languages.

There are a few reasons for *Dracula*'s enduring popularity. One is the sheer amount of research that Stoker put into

The character of Count Dracula may have been inspired by the brutal fifteenth-century Wallachian ruler named Vlad Dracula (pictured). The author incorporated many other historical and geographic facts into his story.

his novel. *Dracula* incorporates many facts about historical figures, geography, vampire legends, and more. The character of Dracula, for instance, may have been partly inspired by an actual Wallachian ruler named Vlad Dracula. Some of the graveyards in Stoker's book are modeled on real places. Lucy Westenra's symptoms before she dies are the true medical signs of blood loss. These facts and many others bring Stoker's tale to life. For readers, this was a welcome change from previous vampire works, which tended to be quickly written and poorly thought out.

Imagining a Monster

Bram Stoker invented many of the features commonly associated with vampires. Here are some of the conventions Stoker dreamed up.

- Vampires cast no shadows or reflections.
- Vampires dislike crucifixes.
- Vampires can change into mist.
- Vampires have mental power over some animals.
- Vampires cannot enter a home unless invited.
- Vampires must sleep on their native soil.
- Vampires cannot cross running water.
- Vampires do not breathe or have a pulse.

Interestingly, Stoker was *not* responsible for the idea that sunlight harms vampires. Count Dracula could function during the daytime, although some of his powers were weaker on sunny days.

Stoker's characters are another reason for *Dracula's* popularity. The people in *Dracula* are well rounded, with their own histories, personalities, and peculiarities. Readers really believed in them. This made *Dracula* an enjoyable read. It also set precedents for future works. Virtually all of Stoker's characters—the demonic villain, the bad-girl victim, the good-girl victim, the vampire hunter, the open-minded doctor, and others—would become archetypes of vampire literature.

Most important of all, of course, is the character of Dracula himself. Stoker did not make his villain just a monster. He made him a memorable monster, with an arsenal of interesting traits and abilities. Dracula can be sophisticated, supernatural, sneaky, or savage, depending on the circumstance. He can turn into fog; he can communicate with animals; he can see in the dark. He can even change the weather. And he manages to have impeccable manners and grooming while doing these things. In short, Dracula is one of the first literary monsters to show any depth of personality—and history rewarded Stoker for this effort.

An Enduring Interest

In Stoker's novel the fictional Dracula may have died, but the character the author created did not. Count Dracula became *the* vampire in most people's minds. His looks, habits, and abilities became the standard against which all other vampires were measured.

Future writers would introduce new ideas, of course. But no one has managed to rock the world of vampire literature like Stoker did with his creepy count. In people's hearts and minds, the word *Dracula* will always conjure thoughts and images of Stoker's masterpiece.

Chapter 2

Toward the Modern Age

Bram Stoker's *Dracula* was a turning point in vampire literature. This book did not just captivate readers. It sparked the imaginations of many writers as well. In the decades after *Dracula*'s publication, more and more vampire-themed works appeared in print.

At first most vampire literature stuck faithfully to the ground rules invented in *Dracula*. But readers soon longed for more original fare. In the mid- to late 1900s, they got it. Authors of this period reimagined and rewrote vampires in many ways. These changes moved the genre of vampire literature into a whole new era.

New Twists

The demon vampire was one invention of this era. Demon vampires are humans possessed by evil spirits. The unlucky humans are helpless vessels for their bloodthirsty masters. This is the case in Sydney Horler's "The Believer: Ten Minutes of Horror." Published in 1935, Horler's short story tells the tale of Joseph Farington, a man whose body is taken over by an unholy entity. The demon forces Farington to drink the blood of young women against his will. This gruesome tale provided one of the earliest links between demonic possession and vampirism.

The "psi" vampire also made its first appearance around this time. Psi vampires act a lot like regular vampires, with one key difference: They do not drink their victims' blood. They suck the life force out of them instead.

Fritz Leiber's "The Girl with the Hungry Eyes" features one of these creatures. Published in 1949, Leiber's classic tale concerns a mysterious fashion model known simply as "the Girl." During the daytime the Girl attends photo shoots. At night she stalks and kills a series of unlucky male victims.

In one passage a photographer remembers how he felt when he worked with the Girl: "I went sort of crazy and light-headed—only sometimes I felt my head was going to burst. And I started to talk to her all the time. About myself. It was like being in a constant delirium. . . . She's the smile that tricks you into throwing away your money and your life. She's the eyes that lead you on and on, and then show you death."[8]

The Girl may have been deadly. But at least she was human in form. Not all authors stuck to this guideline. Some imagined their vampires as bloodsucking beasts instead. This is the premise of E.F. Benson's "Negotium Perambulans" (1922), a classic gore fest that includes this description of an attack by a vampire worm:

> It seemed to have no head, but on the front of it was an orifice of puckered skin which opened and shut and slavered at the edges. It was hairless, and slug-like in shape and texture. As it advanced its fore-part reared itself from the ground, like a snake about to strike,

The 2007 movie I Am Legend, starring Will Smith (pictured), was based on the 1954 novel about the sole human survivor of a plague that turned everyone else on earth into a vampire. The novel was the first major work to link vampirism with science.

and it fastened on [the victim]. . . . There came gurgling and sucking noises, and then it slid out even as it had entered. . . . There on the floor [the victim] lay, no more than a rind of skin in loose folds over projecting bones.[9]

The Legend Reborn

A person could, perhaps, fight off a vampiric worm. But what if the vampire were something as tiny as a germ—unseeable, unstoppable? And what if the germ spread vampirism like a disease? This is the idea behind *I Am Legend*, a novel published in 1954. Written by Richard Matheson, this book stands today as a classic of the vampire genre.

I Am Legend is the tale of Robert Neville, the sole survivor of a plague that has turned every other human on earth into a vampire. Neville spends his days gathering supplies, hanging garlic strands, and killing vampires. At night he barricades himself inside his house and shivers while hungry bloodsuckers pound on his doors and windows.

One day Neville is shocked to meet a woman named

Ruth. Ruth appears to be normal. She eventually reveals, however, that she is indeed a vampire. She tells Neville that the vampires have been learning to control their disease. They are trying to rebuild society. She warns Neville that the other vampires are furious with him, since he has destroyed many of their kind. They plan to capture and kill him.

Neville considers fleeing, but he is tired and lonely. He does not want to live as the only man on earth. He lets himself be captured by a vampire mob. As Neville waits for execution, he realizes that *he* has become the monster. The vampires fear him, just as people used to fear vampires. When Neville dies, he—along with the rest of humanity—will be nothing but a memory. "[I am] a new terror born in death, a new superstition entering the unassailable fortress of forever. I am legend,"[10] he thinks as he dies.

I Am Legend is usually considered the most important vampire tale since *Dracula*. It was the first major work to link vampirism and science. The novel also ditched the creepy atmosphere and adjective-dripping prose of previous vampire literature. By adopting a modern style, it brought vampires another step closer to the modern world.

Strange as It Sounds...
In *Dark Shadows* Barnabas Collins is turned into a vampire after being attacked and bitten by a vampire bat from hell.

Made for TV

It would not take long for another major step to occur. In 1966 the soap opera *Dark Shadows* hit American TV screens. This show focuses on a 200-year-old vampire named Barnabas Collins who shows up one day to terrorize the modern-day Collins family. The show was a huge hit, running for almost five years and eventually including over 1,200 episodes.

In the literary world *Dark Shadows* is important because it spawned something entirely new: the first-ever series of vampire novels. The series was written by author Dan Ross

The television soap opera Dark Shadows, *which began in 1966, featured Barnabas Collins (pictured), a 200-year-old vampire who terrorized his descendants week after week. Collins was also the central character in the Dark Shadows books, although the books told stories not shown on TV.*

under his wife's name. "Marilyn Ross" churned out 33 Dark Shadows novels between December 1966 and March 1972. Sporting titles like *Barnabas Collins vs. the Warlock* and *The Demon of Barnabas Collins*, the hugely popular books feature the familiar characters and locations of the soap opera.

Ross's books do *not*, however, feature the TV show's plot ideas. Each novel tells an all-new story. "I didn't want to imitate other writers. I was willing to use the characters, but when it came to the storyline, I wanted to use my own,"[11] Ross said in a 1990 interview.

This freshness was part of the series' appeal, as Ross well knew. "Other book series . . . copied the storyline on the TV shows, therefore it was rehashed material. When I did the original stories, it was new. It was like giving [people] an extra couple of days to watch the TV show,"[12] explained Ross.

Ross's approach made his series something special. It gave *Dark Shadows* fans even more of their favorite vampires. In doing so, it lured legions of TV watchers into their local bookstores. Word of mouth from these fans attracted other readers. As the years went by, more and more people got their daily dose of vampires in print form—and they liked what they were getting. Thanks in part to *Dark Shadows*, the scene was set for an avalanche of literary vampirism.

A Whole Lot of Vampires

The onslaught began in earnest in 1975 with the publication of Stephen King's second novel, *'Salem's Lot*. Like so many other vampire tales, this one was inspired by *Dracula*. King discusses his lightbulb moment on his official Web site: "One night over supper I wondered aloud what would happen if Dracula came back in the twentieth century, to America.... If he were to show up in a sleepy little country town, what then? I decided I wanted to find out, so I wrote *'Salem's Lot*."[13]

The result was one of King's scariest books. The novel concerns an ancient vampire named Kurt Barlow. Barlow takes up residence in the small Maine town of Jerusalem's Lot, which is usually called 'Salem's Lot for short. Soon after Barlow settles in, the townspeople start to disappear—but not for long. They return as vampires when the sun goes down, thirsty for the blood of their neighbors.

A few people realize what is going on. They band together to hunt and kill Barlow. Although the group loses a few members along the way, it eventually succeeds in its goal. But Barlow's death comes too late to save 'Salem's Lot. The overwhelmed humans are forced to flee, leaving their vampire-infested homes behind.

'Salem's Lot is a very traditional book in many ways. Its story line is a classic humans-versus-monsters tale. The novel also uses most of the conventions established by Bram Stoker—garlic, crucifixes, holy water, coffins, wooden stakes, vampire hypnotism, and so on. In this respect, *'Salem's Lot* offers few surprises.

But King's book is a milestone in vampire literature for

two main reasons. First is the book's setting. King brought one of the most terrifying characters in literary history—Dracula—into the modern world. He made today's readers believe that vampires can be their neighbors and can steal their children in the night. This idea makes *'Salem's Lot* a uniquely terrifying read.

Stephen King himself is the second reason *'Salem's Lot* made such an impact. King's vampire epic was a follow-up to *Carrie*, which was a huge best seller. King's reputation catapulted *'Salem's Lot*—and vampires in general—to formerly unknown heights of popularity.

A Groundbreaking Interview

This trend was cemented in 1976, when yet another vampire classic-to-be hit the shelves. Written by author Anne Rice, the book was called *Interview with the Vampire*. It tells the tale of reluctant vampire Louis and his relationship with his maker/best friend/enemy Lestat de Lioncourt, who is also a vampire.

Rice's fiendish yet surprisingly human characters caught the public's attention. *Interview with the Vampire* was a huge hit in its own right. It also spawned nine sequels, including *The Vampire Lestat*, *The Queen of the Damned*, *The Tale of the Body Thief*, and more. Together, these novels are known as The Vampire Chronicles. Collectively and individually, they are among the best-selling vampire books of all time.

Rice's thoughtful perspective on the vampire condition usually gets the credit for this success. Rice portrays vampirism as a "dark gift" that brings both good and bad to its recipients. On the positive side, her vampires are nearly immortal. They have supernatural powers, and they have heightened senses that make them keenly aware of

Anne Rice

Anne Rice was born Howard Allen O'Brien on October 4, 1941. She chose the name "Anne" for herself when she entered first grade in New Orleans, Louisiana. Her current surname came from her husband, Stan Rice, whom she married in 1961.

Interview with the Vampire was Rice's first book. When she wrote it, says Rice, "I felt that the vampire was the perfect metaphor for the outcast in all of us, the alienated one in all of us, the one who feels lost in a world seemingly without God. In 1976, I felt I existed in such a world, and I was searching for God."

In 2002 Rice found what she was looking for. Feeling a sense of renewed faith, Rice vowed to take a new direction. "I would write works about salvation, as opposed to alienation; I would write books about reconciliation in Christ, rather than books about the struggle for answers," she said.

Today Rice has a large following of Christian readers. But although her audience has changed, Rice's basic approach has not. "My books reflect now, as they always have, what I see and feel and struggle to understand," she says.

Anne Rice, "Essay on Earlier Works," Anne Rice: The Official Site, August 15, 2007. www.annerice.com.

the world's beauty. Most important of all, they can still love and be loved, and their treasured relationships can last for centuries. So in Rice's world, being a vampire can be a very good thing indeed.

But these benefits do not come without cost. Rice's vampires are helpless during the daytime, and they burn to death in sunlight. They are no longer human, and they are outcasts from human society. These facts dismay many of Rice's characters.

Also dismaying is the constant craving for human blood. Some of Rice's vampires accept this need without question. Others, however, find it deeply troubling. They do not want to hurt people. Yet they must feed if they want to stay healthy. In a 1990 interview, Rice explained her thoughts on this dilemma. "To me, a vampire is a tragic figure, someone compelled to do evil when [he] really would rather not. He gets outside of life and sees the absolute beauty of life and yet has to kill to survive,"[14] she says.

Thorny issues like this one drive the action in Rice's books. They also make her vampire characters unforgettable and even sometimes lovable. This quality made The Vampire Chronicles more than just a turning point in vampire literature. It was also a starting point for many of the works that would follow.

Hungry for More

The Hunger (1981) by Whitley Strieber is one of these works. Like Interview with the Vampire, Strieber's novel struggles with some lofty concepts. It uses vampire characters to examine themes of love, longing, ruthlessness, death, and the heartbreaking costs of immortality.

The main character in The Hunger is a vampire named

Miriam Blaylock. Miriam is thousands of years old, and she never ages. She is the last of her kind. As such, she is incredibly lonely. To ease the loneliness, Miriam uses the promise of immortality to lure human lovers to her side. She turns these lovers into temporary vampires, which stops their aging process—for a while. But the effect only lasts two or three centuries. After this period Miriam's lovers age quickly and fall into a never-ending, painful coma. Locked in a dank basement, they live forever in this state while Miriam goes on the hunt for fresh companions.

The Hunger is not a typical vampire novel. Even more than The Vampire Chronicles, it focuses on its characters' thoughts and motives instead of their vampire nature. Some hard-core horror fans find this approach disappointing. "I don't find it frightening. . . . By eliminating the scare factor, the novel metamorphoses from a horror story to a drama. If you're looking for a good vampire novel, look elsewhere,"[15] complains one reader.

Many other people, however, find Strieber's ideas

fascinating. They appreciate the fresh perspective on vampirism and immortality. "The book makes you feel for [Miriam's] loneliness, as the last of her kind, but then reminds you what it means to be loved by her, that you could end up spending eternity rotting conscious in a box," says one reader. "This book is sad, exciting, and scary if you let yourself think about it."[16]

Over the decades, many people have done just that. Strieber's masterpiece confronts readers with the realities of vampirism and makes them feel sympathy for a cold, calculating, and essentially monstrous character. It is a classic trip into the vampire mind that millions of readers have been glad to take.

Making History

Lighter by far, but still captivating to countless fans, is Chelsea Quinn Yarbro's Saint-Germain Cycle. Launched in 1978, this series describes the adventures of an ancient vampire named Count Saint-Germain. It currently includes 24 books, with the most recent one published in 2009.

The success of the Saint-Germain Cycle is due in large part to Yarbro's approach. Yarbro tells her stories in the tradition of historical fiction, setting different books during the Roman Empire, ancient China, World War II–era Europe, and many other times and places. (The count, being nearly 3,500 years old, has had adventures in all of these eras.) Yarbro does a great deal of research to ensure the accuracy of her novels. The result is a mix of history and horror unlike anything else on the market.

Another unique aspect of the Cycle is its lack of chron-ological order. Yarbro bounces with ease from sixteenth-century France to eleventh-century Mongolia, from the

Twisting Traditions

Modern authors tend to pick and choose when it comes to vampire traditions. They keep the conventions they like and abandon those they do not. For example:

- Like Dracula, the vampires of *I Am Legend* roam at night, and they drink blood. But they are far from immortal, and most of them are more like zombies than humans.

- Stephen King's Kurt Barlow follows convention in most ways, with one notable exception: The vampires he creates can survive their maker's death.

- Anne Rice's vampires are virtually immortal, have supernatural powers, and cannot tolerate sunlight. But they have no problem handling crucifixes, holy water, garlic, and other traditional vampire repellents.

- Whitley Strieber's vampires must drink blood, but they do not bite their victims to get it. They must cut the victims with a knife to get their blood flowing.

modern American West to anywhere else her imagination takes her. In terms of setting, therefore, fans of the series never know quite what to expect when a new Saint-Germain novel comes out.

But they do know what to expect from the series' beloved main character, Count Saint-Germain. The vampire count is amazingly pleasant—courtly, attractive, gentle, and startlingly human. These good qualities are no accident. "I did deliberately push the Dracular version of vampires as far to the positive as I could and still have a recognizable vampire,"[17] Yarbro explained in a 2006 interview.

Yarbro also made her count unusually perceptive and open-minded. He constantly questions things, especially those that seem unusual. Yarbro sees this trait as a natural result of the count's immense age and experience. "I think the world is a great deal stranger than we usually allow ourselves to perceive, and since I am writing about a character who is out of time, I would expect him to be aware of that strangeness, his own social context being long gone,"[18] she says.

The count's awareness makes him a memorable character. It also leads him into many occult-tinged adventures. As long as Yarbro's imagination holds out, the count will undoubtedly continue to delight readers everywhere.

Vampires in the Mainstream

The Saint-Germain Cycle and other modern classics are important partly because of the way they redefined vampires. But these novels did much more than that. They brought vampires into the mainstream as well. Today bookstores bulge with vampire-related books for every taste. Young or old, dreamy or dangerous, romantic or occultist, any reader can enjoy the phenomenon of vampire literature.

Strange as It Sounds...

In *The Hunger*, Miriam Blaylock must transfuse her blood into her human lovers to turn them into vampires.

Chapter 3

A Vampire for Every Taste

Most early vampire literature fell squarely into the horror category. *Varney the Vampire*, *Carmilla*, *Dracula*, and even modern classics like *'Salem's Lot* fit this bill perfectly. With their scary story lines and monstrous characters, these works have a time-tested ability to frighten readers.

Vampire horror is still alive and well in the modern age. But it is far from the only genre on the bloodsucking bandwagon. Vampires now star in romances, comedies, children's books, and much more. With so many reading options available, today's literature truly offers a vampire for every taste.

Truly Horrifying

Pure horror, of course, will never go out of style. Today's authors and publishers know this. They produce plenty of terrifying tales that are designed to keep readers awake long into the deep, dark night.

One well-known horror offering is Tanith Lee's Blood Opera Sequence. Published from 1992 to 1994, the three

Most early vampire books, including 'Salem's Lot by Stephen King, were classic horror stories. In a scene from the 1979 television movie version of King's book, a vampire meets his fate at the hands of a vampire hunter.

books in this series tell the tale of the classically creepy Scarabae vampire family. The truth about the clan unfolds through the eyes of Rachaela, who learns at the beginning of the series that she is a Scarabae daughter. Disturbing and downright frightening things start to happen soon afterward.

Lee's sense of the macabre makes the Blood Opera Sequence an exciting read. In an online review, one reader praises the books for their "excellent usage of sinister prose combined with a sense of building horror."[19] This is the type of feeling that old-school vampire fans love, and Lee's books are enduringly popular as a result.

Another creepy tale with plenty of traditional flair is *They Hunger* (2007) by Scott Nicholson. This novel concerns batlike vampires that erupt from the underworld after a landslide opens long-hidden caves. The vampires terrorize a West Virginia rafting expedition, picking off its unlucky human members one by one.

Nicholson's novel is not terribly subtle or original. But this is no problem for the book's many fans, who love the author's no-holds-barred horror approach. "One aspect I liked about these vampires is [that they] are killing machines, pure and simple. The fact that their origins and motivations are never explained just makes the whole thing more nightmarish,"[20] says one enthusiastic reader. For this person and many others, simple is good when it comes to vampire fare.

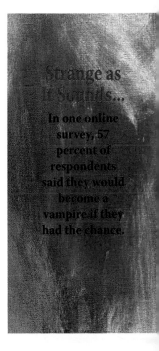

Strange as It Sounds...

In one online survey, 57 percent of respondents said they would become a vampire if they had the chance.

Blending Old and New

But the original approach still earns points, too, as shown by the 2007 best seller *Fangland*. Written by John Marks, this novel is in some ways a modern-day retelling of *Dracula*. It concerns a TV news producer who travels to Romania for

Dracula, the Sequel

Many authors have used Bram Stoker's Dracula as a character in their work. No writer, however, has been as uniquely qualified to do so as Dacre Stoker, Bram's great-grandnephew and the coauthor of *Dracula: The Un-Dead* (2007). This best-selling book is a sequel to *Dracula*. Based on Bram's actual notes, it is meant to extend and celebrate the original novel's vision.

In a 2009 interview, Dacre Stoker discussed the idea behind his work:

> Other authors have used some of Bram's original characters. Some have done a better job than others. I feel what separates *Dracula the Un-Dead* is that we not only recreated, but extended, these characters in the manner which Bram might have, if *Dracula* was not written in the journal form. We provide the reader with back stories involving the relationships between the central characters, which we believe are true to Bram's work.

The result is an all-new Dracula tale that is unfailingly faithful to the original. This approach has proved to be popular among die-hard Dracula fans. It has also attracted new readers, as Dacre Stoker hoped it would.

Quoted in James J. Gormley, "Exclusive Interview with Dacre Stoker," Vampire Books Navigator, October 12, 2009. http://vampirebooksnavigator.blogspot.com.

a story, only to be imprisoned by a vampire in a hotel penthouse. The producer eventually escapes and returns to her New York life, but discovers that the vampire has followed. Death, mayhem, and other bad things soon follow.

Fans of the original *Dracula* appreciate *Fangland*'s blend of old and new themes. "The best thing about this book is that it takes the thread of an idea that has been so overworked and actually makes the idea riveting and fresh in a new skin,"[21] says one reader.

Of course, as this reader points out, the book is full of frightening moments as well. "*Fangland* offers you many gifts as a reader [including] mounting, suffocating dread and truly shocking horror,"[22] he says. This quality earns *Fangland* and other classically creepy books a spot on every horror fan's must-read list.

Love Bites

Some readers cannot stomach the guts-and-gore approach. They prefer hearts and flowers instead. A thriving vampire romance industry caters to these readers.

Vampire romances tend to be more popular among women than men. It is no surprise, then, that romantic vampires are usually male. They are generally attractive, sometimes stunningly so. They are suave and sophisticated. Some romantic vampires are witty, the "unlife" of the party. Others are dark and brooding. But whatever their personalities, there is just *something* about them. They are the ultimate bad boys, oozing a sense of danger that fictional women seem to find irresistible.

In a 2006 article, one romance editor discussed the appeal of vampire romance. Vampires, she says, "have been alive for 600 years. They've experienced everything. Then all of a sudden they meet this great heroine, who basically is a breath of fresh air. Falling in love, trying to find that spark again in their lives—that is a great romantic fantasy. They do suck blood, but it's a very erotic process."[23]

Author Christine Feehan uses this theme to good effect in her Dark series, which is one of the most successful franchises in the romantic vampire genre. The 20 novels in this cycle concern the Carpathians, a powerful and ancient vampire clan. All of the female Carpathians have died out. This situation forces male Carpathians to seek "lifemates" among the human population. The result is tale after tale of vampire-human love, longing, salvation, and, of course, lust—lots of it.

Similar concepts run through author Nancy Gideon's popular Midnight series. In this nine-novel set, various human-vampire couples struggle and fail to overcome their forbidden attraction. The marketing text for these books is ripped straight from the romance tradition. "Laure Cristobel became a bride out of necessity; to protect herself and the unborn child she carries. Though alarmed to find herself wed to a monster, she's dangerously close to falling in love with the man he once was . . . the man she hopes she can make him once again,"[24] gushes a typical blurb.

Plotlines like this one leave many readers swooning with delight. Sure, romantic vampires may be fiends. But they have all the desires of mortal men, and they can be enslaved by the right woman. It is a powerful fantasy that never seems to grow old. As long as women dream of finding "Mr. Right," the vampire romance genre will continue to feed these flames.

Funny Stuff

Among the undead, love tends to be serious business. Vampire romance, therefore, can be pretty heavy reading.

Strange as It Sounds...
Dracula himself sets the record straight in Fred Saberhagen's amusing *The Dracula Tape* (1992). The vampire claims he was framed and tries to convince readers that he is not such a bad guy after all.

Comics with a Biting Edge

Many vampire tales have been printed in graphic-novel format. The classic series *Vampirella* (1969–1983) concerns a vampiric space vixen. *I . . . Vampire* (1981–1983) follows the adventures of Andrew Bennett, a good vampire who is trying to destroy an evil vampire clan. And *The Tomb of Dracula* (1972–1979) features a group of vampire hunters who fight Dracula and other supernatural menaces. This series also launched the half-human/half-vampire character Blade, who went on to star in several comic series of his own and, eventually, a blockbuster movie of the same name.

The graphic-novel format is still popular today. Current noteworthy series include Vampire Knight with its pureblood vampire princess, Yuuki Cross; Blood Alone, a vampire serial with crime-adventure themes; and Chibi Vampire, a Japanese series about a vampire named Karin who has a very unusual problem. This "backward" vampire produces too much blood and must bite others to release it.

Graphic novels are printed in comic book format. This makes them very popular among young readers. But graphic novels are not just for kids. With their complex story lines and visual punch, these supernatural tales attract fans of all ages.

But a few authors have ditched the drama in favor of a humorous approach. They have written books that try to see the funny side of vampire love and life.

MaryJanice Davidson's Queen Betsy series is one standout in this genre. In the series' first book, *Undead and Unwed*, a young woman named Betsy awakes in a coffin dressed in a tacky pink dress and—the horror!—cheap shoes. Betsy soon discovers that she has become a vampire. But life—or, in Betsy's case, the afterlife—goes on. Friends, romance, shopping, and designer footwear are still the top worries on Betsy's list. Now if only she could conquer that pesky craving for blood.

Since 2004, when the first Queen Betsy book was published, readers have flocked to Davidson's series. Fans enjoy the fact that Betsy is shallow, silly, vain, and completely unbothered by her vampiric transformation. "Sometimes in this genre the books tend to be very dark, and although I enjoy those as well, it's nice to get a 'breath of fresh air' and be able to read a book with a good balance of humor along with the darkness,"[25] says one happy reader.

Many people feel the same way about Christopher Moore's *Bloodsucking Fiends* (1995) and its sequel, *You Suck* (2006). In these laugh-out-loud-funny best sellers, new vampire Jody and her human boyfriend, Tommy, try to navigate the vampire life. They cope with the club scene, shoe-eating turtles, and turkey-bowling grocery clerks, all while tracking the evil vampire who is trying to frame Jody for a series of murders.

Books like these provide plenty of chuckles. They also breathe new life into vampires by making these most traditional of monsters sympathetic and even fun. And to many readers, fun is exactly what a good book should be all about.

Sci-Fi Suckers

Not all people feel this way. Some read to discover new worlds, societies, creatures, and ways of thinking. The field of vampire science fiction has a lot to offer these readers. From alternate realities to alien vampires, today's novels describe close encounters of every imaginable vampire kind.

Colin Wilson's *The Space Vampires* (1976) is an early example of vampire science fiction and still one of the best known. This novel is set in the mid-twenty-first century, when humankind has become proficient at space travel. A group of astronauts finds several dead humans aboard an enormous, seemingly abandoned alien spaceship. They take the bodies back to earth, only to discover that they are neither human nor dead. They are actually space vampires that feed on the life energy of other beings. When one of the vampires escapes, scientists must track it down before the body count gets too high—and before the alien can invite more space vampires to populate the earth.

In more recent years, E.E. Knight's Vampire Earth series has found a large audience. Published from 2003 to 2009, the eight books in this series describe a future in which the earth is controlled by the Kurian race. The Kurians are vampiric beings that feed on human energy. To get this energy, they form psychic bonds with monstrous creatures called Reapers. The Reapers attack humans and pierce their hearts with long, sharp tongues. As they drain the victims' blood, the Reapers ingest their life force as well. They telepathically transfer this force to their Kurian masters.

Fans of The Vampire Earth books love the author's unique blend of horror, science fiction, and action. Hardcore vampire fans also appreciate the series' original approach

Strange as It Sounds...

Some therapists think women turn to vampire romance because it makes them feel safe. Vampire boyfriends are much more powerful than humans and can do whatever it takes to protect their soul mates.

to a classic legend. "All the great stories have been told. . . . Finding a really good vampire novel that doesn't rehash old matter is a rare treat, and that's why I enjoyed [this series]," [26] says one reader.

Ghoulish Grab Bag

Science fiction fans are not the only readers who feel this way, of course. Fresh ideas can spice up any type of story—and vampires seem to be the perfect seasoning. Today these mythical monsters are popping up in every imaginable literary genre.

Take the medical thriller, for example. In Steven Spruill's *Rulers of Darkness* (1998), a detective and a doctor team up to track a homicidal maniac. The pair use medical techniques to uncover a shocking fact: The killer has a rare disease that causes an uncontrollable craving for fresh blood. Will they stop the vampire in time? Can they cure him? And will the doctor discover the detective's dark secret—that he himself is also a vampire? These questions are answered in classic medical-whodunit style, with enough fast-paced action to keep readers turning the pages.

For police/action/adventure fans, David Wellington's Laura Caxton novels may contain a better prescription. Published between 2007 and 2009, the four books in this series concern detective-turned-vampire-hunter Laura Caxton. Caxton copes with legions of bloodthirsty fiends in fast-paced story lines that pit police officer against vampire. "Minimally plotted and driven by nonstop action," [27] as one review puts it, these books leave readers breathless and hungry for more.

Slower-paced but more delicious to the academically minded is *The Historian* (2005), by Elizabeth Kostova. Kostova's best-selling novel describes one woman's quest to find the real

Dracula. It is hard-core historical fiction, loaded with dates, facts, and carefully researched descriptions of real-world locations. The book's action sequences involve more library-snooping than vampire-busting. This feature makes Kostova's work boring to some readers. But hundreds of thousands of fans disagree. *The Historian* shot to the top of the *New York Times* best-seller list upon its publication, becoming one of the most successful vampire novels of all time.

A Flexible Figure

When it comes to literature, vampires are the ultimate changelings. They can fit in anywhere. This is probably because vampires can symbolize so many different concepts and feelings. Lisa Lampert-Weisseg, professor of literature at the University of California–San Diego, explains it this way:

> The [vampire] figure is so powerful because it's so flexible. Vampires are dead and alive, they're human and not human. They're immortal, so they have time and history on their side. But they've had human lives and so they have that possibility for connection with the reader and with the audience. They're really [thought provoking] because they . . . transcend a lot of boundaries and do a lot of things that ordinary humans can't do.[28]

With all these qualities, vampires are blank slates. They can play any role an author desires. It is no wonder that these imaginary fiends are hiding in every corner of today's bookstores and libraries, ready to leap off the shelves and into readers' nightmares.

Too Big for One Book

No discussion of vampire genres would be complete without a look at the biggest phenomenon of them all: the big-name, blockbuster vampire series. Many modern authors are earning fame and fortune in this field. They have borrowed ideas from many genres to create vampiric characters and worlds that are much too big for one book.

Laurell K. Hamilton's Anita Blake, Vampire Hunter series is among the most popular of these offerings. The heroine of these novels, Anita Blake, is a human law-enforcement agent in a world where vampires, zombies, werewolves, and other mythical beings run rampant. Blake has many supernatural abilities, including the power to raise the dead. In the series' early books, she uses this ability and others mostly to keep nonhuman criminals in line. As the series progresses through 19 installments, Blake slowly becomes less and less human herself.

Heroine-confronts-supernatural is also a theme in Tanya Huff's Blood series. The five-book Blood cycle concerns private investigator Vicki Nelson, who has resigned from the police force. In the first book Nelson meets vampire Henry Fitzroy while investigating a vampire-like murder. The two form a partnership that develops into romance as the series moves on. They must juggle this relationship while fighting to overcome the evil forces that are running amok in the city. This complicated scenario keeps readers guessing. It also makes the Blood cycle one of the best-loved vampire series of all time.

Just as popular but more real in tone is Charlaine Harris's Southern Vampire series. This 10-book masterwork is set in modern-day Louisiana, with one important change. In *this* Louisiana—as in the rest of the world—humans are trying to coexist with vampires, werewolves, fairies, and other mythical beings. This arrangement is possible thanks to a newly developed blood substitute called TruBlood, which makes it unnecessary for vampires to feed on people. This means humanity is safe from its oldest enemy. Or is it? Trying to answer this question leads heroine Sookie Stackhouse into endless trouble and, of course, love—of the vampire variety.

In a 2008 article, TV producer Alan Ball discusses the appeal of Harris's novels. "Charlaine has just created this amazing world that's funny and vibrant and scary and also a sort of social treatise," he says. "The books are violent and that's part of the appeal. It's visceral and predatory and unapologetically sexual. And it's unapologetically romantic in the sense of an old-fashioned romance novel."[29]

This mixture of qualities has proved to be a winning recipe. The Southern Vampire series has attracted countless fans and has spawned a small empire of offshoots, including a hit TV show. It is yet another example of the vampire's seemingly endless ability to shock, thrill, and captivate audiences of all types.

New Blood

There are thousands of other vampire-related titles—enough to keep even the most rabid fans busy for a lifetime. Yet there is no sign of a slowdown. Publishers in every genre continue to produce vampire literature, and readers continue to flock to these works. They have been bitten by the vampire bug, and they are hungry for more. As long as this is the case, new blood will continue to flow in the world of vampire literature.

Chapter 4

Twilight and Beyond: Vampires in Teen Literature

As recently as a few decades ago, vampires were considered adults-only fare. While teens were certainly devouring the works of Stephen King, Anne Rice, and other popular authors, they were not the intended audience. Nearly all vampire novels were written and published with adult readers in mind.

This is no longer the case. Today teen-oriented vampire literature is one of the most successful segments of the publishing industry. Rows upon rows of vampire works line the teen section of most bookstores. From funny to serious, angst-ridden to awful, these works are breathing new life into an old yet ageless topic.

Twilight Falls

Any discussion of teen literature has to start with Stephenie Meyer's Twilight series, the modern-day champion of the vampire genre. This series includes four books: *Twilight* (2005), *New Moon* (2006), *Eclipse* (2007), and *Breaking Dawn* (2008). Individually and as a group, these novels have

captivated countless teens and more than a few adults, too.

The Twilight series is told mostly from the viewpoint of a teenager named Bella Swan. When the series opens, Bella is leaving her mother's home in Arizona to live with her father in Forks, Washington. As far as Bella can tell, the rain never stops in this small, boring town. Bella is miserably unhappy about this fact and many others, and she is feeling very depressed about her new life.

Everything changes, though, when Bella meets the stunningly attractive Edward Cullen at school. Edward and Bella get to know one another. Before long, they have fallen deeply in love. Bella soon learns the disturbing truth about her new boyfriend: He is a 104-year-old vampire, and the rest of his "family" are vampires as well. The Cullens live and walk among humans, and they do not prey on the people around them. They drink animal blood instead.

The four-book Twilight series by Stephenie Meyer has captured the hearts of teens (and some adults too). In a scene from the 2008 movie version of the first book, Twilight, *the vampire Edward Cullen and the human teenager Bella Swan meet.*

But the Cullens are far from immune to the scent of human blood. They still crave this precious liquid. At first this fact creates a dilemma for Edward. Should he kiss Bella, or should he rip her neck open? These conflicting desires place Bella in constant danger from her vampiric suitor, as described in this typical passage:

> His mouth lingered on mine, cold and smooth and gentle, until I wrapped my arms around his neck and threw myself into the kiss with a little too much enthusiasm. I could feel his lips curve upward as he let go of my face and reached back to unlock my grip on him.
>
> Edward had drawn many careful lines for our physical relationship, with the intent being to keep me alive. Though I respected the need for maintaining a safe distance between my skin and his razor-sharp, venom-coated teeth, I tended to forget about trivial things like that when he was kissing me.[30]

Luckily for Bella, Edward has excellent self-control. He decides early on that he will never do anything to harm his true love. Other vampires, however, do not feel the same way. As Meyer's story progresses through four thick books, Bella faces peril after life-threatening peril. Will she survive? Will her relationship with Edward continue to thrive? And will she finally get what she wants most: to become a vampire herself? These questions and others keep readers turning pages, from the series' opening paragraph to its satisfyingly drama-drenched conclusion.

A Publishing Phenomenon

Although *Twilight* was well received when it first hit bookstores in 2005, it was not an instant sensation. It took time to build an audience. As more and more readers learned of Meyer's vampiric world, they fell desperately in love with Edward and Bella. They could not wait to read more of the mismatched lovers' story. By the time *New Moon* was released a year later, full-blown fan mania was poised to erupt.

Publisher Megan Tingley remembers the moment she realized she had a phenomenon on her hands. She was at a bookstore with Meyer for a signing event. "The kids had been cutting school to get these tickets and waiting in line forever. When Stephenie came out, these girls next to me started trembling and crying and grabbing each other," she recalls. "It was crazy . . . it was like the newsreels of the Beatles or Elvis."[31]

Recent sales of the Twilight series reflect this hysteria. In 2008 the four novels claimed the top four spots on *USA Today*'s year-end best-seller list. Meyer was the first author ever to accomplish this feat. By the end of 2009, the four novels as a group had sold about 85 million copies worldwide. There are many reasons for this success. Teens love the Twilight series partly because it focuses on issues that are important in their own lives. They identify with Meyer's themes of sexual longing, alienation, and the struggle to fit in. They also like the idea of the dorky girl capturing the attention of the coolest boy in school—who just happens, in this case, to be a vampire.

All of these themes could be explored without throwing vampires into the mix. But in the Twilight series, the vampire element definitely raises the stakes. It turns a standard teen-angst, coming-of-age story into something sinister, thrilling,

Strange as It Sounds...

The vampires in Melissa de la Cruz's Blue Bloods series are fallen angels who have repented but are doomed to spend eternity as vampires.

Fang Fiction

By the end of a book or series, readers feel like they really know the characters involved. It can be hard to give up these "friendships" when a novel ends. A thriving field called *fan fiction* tries to fill this void.

As the term suggests, fan fiction is written by fans. It features familiar characters, situations, and settings, but it generally tackles all-new issues. What would happen if Bella dumped Edward? What if the Vampire Academy was forced to accept humans? What if Melissa de la Cruz's Blue Bloods heroine developed a killer case of acne? These and other burning questions were not addressed by the characters' original creators. But they can be explored in delightful depth by anyone with the imagination and time to spare.

Fan fiction exists in all literary genres. It is explosively popular, however, in the vampire realm. In early 2010, one Web site listed fan fiction related to dozens of series, including The Vampire Diaries, Vampire Academy, Blue Bloods, and The Vampire Earth. On the same site, Twilight alone had generated almost 90,000 works of fan fiction.

Different authors have different feelings about this phenomenon. Twilight's Stephenie Meyer encourages it. She even posts links to fan-fiction sites on her official Web page. The Vampire Chronicles' Anne Rice, on the other hand, has fought against fan fiction for decades. She has even taken legal action against sites that post such work.

and sensual. In doing so, it has piqued teens' interests in all things vampire.

More Paranormal Romance

The Twilight effect has been especially strong in the teen romance genre. Today tales of youthful vampire/human love are everywhere. Usually featuring undead young men and human young women, these stories never seem to lose their appeal.

L.J. Smith's Night World series is one popular entry in this field. Originally published from 1996 to 1998, these books have enjoyed a Twilight-fueled revival in recent years. The series' premise is that vampires and other supernatural creatures live among humans while belonging to a super-secret society called the Night World. Members of the Night World are not allowed to become entangled with humans. But this rule is constantly tested when young human women meet their male vampire "soul mates." Forbidden love and extreme peril are the inevitable results.

The premise of the series is summarized in an exchange from *Secret Vampire*, the first Night World novel. James, who is a vampire, is talking with Poppy, his human love.

> James's grey eyes met hers, and there was a look in them Poppy couldn't remember seeing before. "There are two cardinal rules in the Night World," he said steadily. "One is not to tell humans that it exists. The other is not to fall in love with a human. I've broken both of them. . . . It puts you in terrible danger."
>
> "And you, too," Poppy said. It was the first time she'd really thought about this. Now the

idea emerged from her muddled conscious-
ness like a bubble in a pot of stew. "I mean . . .
if it's against the rules to tell a human or love
a human, and you break the rules, then there
must be some punishment for *you*."[32]

Poppy is right. There are terrible consequences for
vampires who break the rules. But the call of true love is
impossible to resist. In book after book of the Night World
series, young male vampires risk everything for the young
women they adore.

The theme of dangerous love is central to the hugely
popular Vampire Diaries novels as well. Also written by
L.J. Smith, this series concerns a young woman named
Elena and the vampire brothers, Stefan and Damon, who
compete for her affection. Elena is drawn to Stefan at first,
but she is increasingly torn between the brothers as the
series progresses. This love triangle creates a great deal of
tension. It also leads the threesome into many dangerous
and supernatural situations.

Like Smith's Night World series, the Vampire Diaries
books were only moderately popular in their first run in
the early 1990s. They were an immediate hit, however,
upon their rerelease in 2007. The time was clearly right for
Elena, Stefan, and Damon to unleash their species-crossing
romance on the world of teen literature.

Dying to Be Popular

Romance is not the only issue on teens' minds. Many middle
and high school students are also worried about popularity.
They think endlessly about who has it, who does not, and
how to get it or keep it themselves. Vampire literature offers

a perfect way to explore this theme.

It is not hard to see why vampires can be such a strong metaphor for popularity. In writers' imaginations, these beings become supernaturally attractive and confident. They are often rich. They seem to have more freedom than human teens, with very little parental oversight. They often form close-knit and highly desirable vampire cliques that humans cannot penetrate. All of these facts combine to make teen vampires the coolest of the cool.

This is the case in Nancy A. Collins's VAMPS series (2009), which takes place at the super-exclusive Bathory Academy for teenage vampires. The books' central clique is a group of vampires who look and live like Hollywood celebrities. One of the vampires, Lilith, is the classic mean young woman with a bloodthirsty twist. "I just took your basic self-absorbed, insecure, high-maintenance high school rich [girl] and added the fact she's a, you know, shape-shifting, blood-drinking MONSTER to the mix,"[33] laughs Collins in an online interview.

Melissa de la Cruz's Blue Bloods series (2007–2010) takes a similar approach. Like VAMPS, Blue Bloods focuses on an exclusive private school. The school's most popular students are known as the "Blue Bloods." They are wealthy, powerful, and gorgeous. Unknown to most of the student body, they are also vampires.

The series takes off when two seemingly regular students, Schuyler and Bliss, reach age 15 and start to turn into vampires. The two young vampires are quickly initiated into the Blue Blood crowd. They must learn the ways of vampire life while struggling to fit in with their glamorous new friends. Designer clothing, high-end shopping, limo rides, society parties, and even a vampire fashion show play

Strange as It Sounds...

The vampires in the Cirque du Freak series can exhale an invisible gas that renders humans unconscious.

prominent roles in these tales of New York's secret vampire aristocracy.

Less trendy but just as socially challenged are the characters in Ellen Schreiber's Vampire Kisses series (2007–2009). These books feature a goth girl named Raven who is a complete social outcast at school. Everything changes when Raven starts dating a new boy named Alexander. With Alexander by her side, Raven does not feel so alone. She is also thrilled to discover that her boyfriend is a vampire, which she thinks is the best thing ever. Who needs to fit in with the human crowd when hanging out with vampires is an option?

Tales of Growing Up

The vampire gang is not always so alluring for characters who actually *are* vampires. Teen literature is full of stories about young men and women who are either vampires by birth or whose lives change after they are "turned." In these books, coping with vampirism reflects teens' concerns about growing up and learning to deal with the adult world.

This concern is evident in Richelle Mead's popular Vampire Academy series (2007–2010). In these books, different types of young vampires live and study together at St. Vladimir's Academy. Some of the teen vampires are royalty-in-training. Others are learning to be bodyguards for the royal set. All of the students know they will assume life-or-death responsibilities after they graduate. In the meantime, however, they must cope with schoolwork, romantic entanglements, popularity issues, and other classic teen problems.

Life change is also the basis of the Saga of Darren Shan (also known as the Cirque du Freak) series (2000–2009). The 12 books in this series are written from the viewpoint

of Darren Shan, a fictional teen who is listed as the books' author. In the series' first book, *A Living Nightmare*, Shan begs a vampire to save his friend's life. He allows himself to be turned into a half-vampire in return. He quickly discovers that the vampire world is very different from the human world—and much more dangerous, too. Shan must grow up quickly in order to cope with his new circumstances.

In *The Vampire's Assistant*, the second book in the series, Shan discusses his feelings about his new identity: "It had been almost two months since my 'death,' but I was having a tough time adjusting to the change. It was hard to believe my old way of life was finished, that I was a half-vampire and could never go back. I knew I had to eventually leave my human life behind. But it was easier said than done."[34]

Shan misses his parents, his little sister, and his friends above all other things. Teens can identify with these feelings. They care deeply about their friends, and they know how hard it would be to lose them. They also expect to be moving out of their parents' homes within a few years, and they anticipate how hard *that* will be, too. They are therefore very sympathetic to Shan's plight. The fact that Shan gets amazing vampire powers along with these problems adds supernatural thrills to a familiar situation.

The Younger Set Gets Sucked In, Too

The darker elements of teen literature can be a bit much for younger readers. But these days, middle schoolers and even elementary school students are interested in vampires. A growing body of vampire books with lighter themes caters to this crowd. The vampires in these books are not very scary. They tend to be regular kids with regular problems.

This is the case in Todd Strasser's *Help! I'm Trapped in*

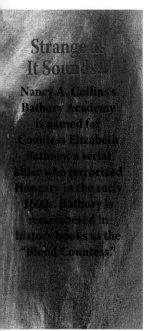

Strange as It Sounds...

Nancy A. Collins's *Bathory Academy* is named for Countess Elizabeth Báthory, a serial killer who terrorized Hungary in the early 1600s. Báthory is remembered in history books as the "Blood Countess."

a Vampire's Body (2000). In this book, eighth-grader Jake accidentally absorbs a vampire's powers after being zapped with a machine in the school science lab. Jake uses his newfound abilities to defeat bullies, conquer his opponents in a toilet-paper fight, and change into a bat. He is occasionally tempted to bite his friends' necks. But he just chugs some blood-red vegetable juice to fend off this bothersome urge. No harm is ever done, and there is virtually no scare factor to keep readers up at night.

The scares are also few and far between in Sienna Mercer's popular My Sister the Vampire series (2007–2010). These books focus on cheerleader Olivia and goth Ivy, eighth-grade

The idea for Twilight *came to author Stephenie Meyer (pictured) in a dream. In Meyer's dream, a vampire boy desperately fought the urge to attack a human girl whom he loved.*

Stephenie Meyer's "Fangtastic" Dream

On June 2, 2003, stay-at-home mom Stephenie Meyer awoke from an unusually vivid dream. In the dream, Meyer had seen a human girl and a vampire boy standing in a flowery meadow. The vampire was sparkling in the sunlight. Meyer sensed that he wanted to attack the girl. But he loved her, so he was resisting with all his might.

This idea intrigued Meyer. She thought about her dream all day long. By the time evening arrived, she felt compelled to write it down. "[I] put everything that I possibly could on the back burner and sat down at the computer to write—something I hadn't done in so long that I wondered why I was bothering," she remembers. "But I didn't want to lose the dream."

Three months later the manuscript for *Twilight*—which prominently featured the meadow scene from Meyer's dream—was complete. The manuscript soon found an agent, then a publisher. The completed novel hit stores in October 2005 and quickly climbed to number 5 on the *New York Times* best-seller list. It was followed in rapid succession by the sequels *New Moon* (September 2006) and *Eclipse* (August 2007). The final book in the series, *Breaking Dawn*, sold 1.3 million copies within 24 hours of its release on August 2, 2008, making Meyer one of the most successful authors of all time.

Stephenie Meyer, "The Story Behind Twilight," official Web site of Stephenie Meyer. www.stepheniemeyer.com.

girls who meet after Olivia transfers to a new school. Olivia and Ivy soon discover that they are twin sisters, separated at birth. They also find out that Olivia is human, while Ivy is a vampire. But this fact does not deter the sisters' friendship. Olivia and Ivy juggle peer pressure, a secret vampire society, cheerleading crises, and more, all while keeping their promise to stick together no matter what.

The preteen vampire siblings of Adele Griffin's Vampire Island series (2008–2010) find strength in numbers, too. Lexie, Hudson, and Maddy have left their vampire lives in Europe behind and moved to New York City. They worry mostly about recycling, fitting in, and making new friends. They are no danger to their new human friends since they are partly fruit bats and eat only plant matter. The result is a "cuddly, friendly vampire story with nary a (human) death,"[35] as one reviewer puts it.

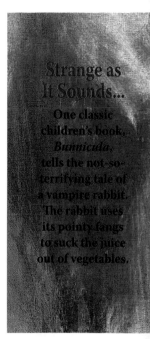

Strange as It Sounds...

One classic children's book, *Bunnicula*, tells the not-so-terrifying tale of a vampire rabbit. The rabbit uses its pointy fangs to suck the juice out of vegetables.

An Enduring Interest

Vampire-related children's books may seem pointless to readers who enjoy the fear factor. But they serve an important purpose in the world of vampire literature. They introduce novice readers to the vampire mystique in a not-too-scary way. Children who love elementary-level vampire books may eventually move on to teen vampire literature.

There are no statistics to prove this progression. But sales figures *do* prove that today's teens are endlessly interested in reading about vampires. In the end, it does not really matter how or why this obsession started. As long as this situation continues, teen readers will have countless choices in the field of vampire literature.

Chapter 5

More than Just a Good Read

Vampires are notoriously hard to pin down. They easily escape from human foes, locked rooms, and other sticky situations. Because they are immortal, or nearly so, they can even cheat death. It should be no surprise, then, that vampires have managed a type of reincarnation as well. They have left the books where they were born to find new lives on TV and movie screens everywhere.

Not all fictional vampires find their way onto film, of course. But many novels and series have made the leap. Between the early 1900s and the present, vampire literature has inspired some very popular films and TV shows.

Twilight Fever

The most popular offering of all is also one of the most recent. The movie version of Stephenie Meyer's *Twilight* hit big screens everywhere in November 2008. The film was an instant smash, earning nearly $70 million in its opening weekend. It went on to earn about $385 million worldwide during its theater run, making *Twilight* one of the 100 top-grossing movies of all time.

This success pales in comparison to the second film

installment in the *Twilight* saga. *New Moon* took in an incredible $143 million in its first 3 days of release. Between November 2009 and February 2010, the movie took in more than $700 million worldwide. It reached the $100 million mark faster than any previous film and went on to become the thirty-third highest grossing movie in history.

And the story does not stop there. *Eclipse* and *Breaking Dawn*, the third and fourth books in Meyer's series, were also scheduled for film release. With *Twilight* fever still soaring, there is a good chance that they, too, will reach blockbuster status.

In Love with Rob and Kristen

The numbers prove that *Twilight* and *New Moon* are popular. But this popularity is not without controversy. Many fervent fans of the series feel that the films do not follow the books closely enough. They think that important scenes and details have been left out. They also do not like the fact that some elements have been added.

What fans *do* like, almost universally, is the movie's cast. They appreciate Bella, who is played by a young actress named Kristen Stewart. "Stewart brings a beautiful and nuanced performance. She is exactly how I pictured Bella and she does an excellent job of bringing the character to life,"[36] says one enthusiastic viewer.

The real draw of the Twilight films, however, is Edward Cullen. Cullen is played by Robert Pattinson, an English actor who started out with a small role in a Harry Potter movie. Handsome, intense, and brooding, Pattinson gives off the ultimate bad-boy vibe. He portrays Edward Cullen and all things vampire in a way that makes many teenage girls swoon with desire.

Strange as It Sounds...
Between 2009 and 2010 more than 30 vampire books were being made into movies.

One teenager admits to this yearning in an online chat forum. "I was ecstatic when they chose [Robert]. In my mind, he is the perfect Edward. His tousled bronze hair, those liquid topaz eyes, that perfect crooked smile. . . . I have to stop myself before I look like an overobsessed fan girl. ROB ROB ROB ROB ROB! Oops, too late,"[37] she writes.

Another young fan takes the obsession a step further. "I really don't know what I would be doing with my life without Rob. 'Cause most of the stuff I think/say/type/do relates to him in some way. . . .He really is gorgeous!"[38] she gushes.

This attraction is partly a result of Pattinson's appearance. But moviegoers say good looks are only part of the draw. Pattinson is portraying a good-looking vampire, which makes him much more interesting than any regular high-school hunk. He is also putting a face on a much-loved literary character. Even before the *Twilight* movie came out, millions of young women already adored Edward. Pattinson's performance just gives them a little bit more to love.

More Teens on Screen

It is not surprising that *Twilight*'s success caught Hollywood's attention. Before long another popular teen vampire series found its way onto the big screen. *Cirque du Freak: The Vampire's Assistant* was released in October 2009. This movie covers the first three books of Darren Shan's saga and leaves the door open for possible sequels.

The Vampire's Assistant had all the ingredients of a hit. It featured several big-name stars, including John C. Reilly, Salma Hayek, and Willem Dafoe. Chris Massoglia, the actor who played Darren Shan, was young and attractive. The movie included plenty of action scenes, and it got a good

marketing push from its studio. And, of course, it was about vampires.

Despite these many positives, *The Vampire's Assistant* got lukewarm reviews, and it did only so-so at the box office. Still, most Cirque du Freak fans loved the film. They liked its vision and the way it brought Shan's novels to life. They also appreciated its story line, which offered a unique perspective on the vampire world. "I have watched many Vampire movies in my day and this had to be one of the most original! I was blown away. . . . A definite must see,"[39] writes one satisfied viewer.

Drac Attack

Not all moviegoers feel this way. Many vampire fans have no interest in originality. They would rather watch films that bring traditional tales and monsters to life. And when it comes to vampires, nothing could be more traditional than Dracula. The granddaddy of the bloodsucking bunch, Stoker's vampiric count has terrified millions of shivering movie fans over the decades.

The first Dracula-inspired movie appeared in 1931. Titled simply *Dracula*, this film was a fairly faithful adaptation of Bram Stoker's novel. It was tame by today's horror-movie standards. At the time, though, it was the spookiest film most people had ever seen. "I lived in the era shortly after this movie was released. When I watched it on the screen when I was a kid, it scared the living bejabbers out of me,"[40] recalls one man.

There were many things to like about *Dracula*. The film had the book's good plot and interesting characters. It also had consistently creepy scenery. But fans agree that the best thing about the film was Count Dracula himself.

Played by a Hungarian actor named Bela Lugosi, the movie count was handsome and charming, yet also menacing and evil. Lugosi's performance was so frightening that some audience members reportedly fainted during *Dracula*'s 1931 premiere.

Lugosi's real impact, though, was much larger than a few fainting spells. Film historians agree that Lugosi did not merely play Dracula. He *became* Dracula, creating a memorable character that audiences would forever link with Stoker's fictional vampire. "Even today, when the character of Dracula comes to mind, we are more likely to think of Lugosi than any other actor that later played the role,"[41] reads one recent commentary.

Considering that scores of actors have tackled the part of Dracula, this is a tall order indeed. But no movie has captured the vampire-loving public's imagination like the 1931 original. With his aristocratic bearing, heavy accent, and piercing gaze, Lugosi made an impression that will never fade.

Re-Vamping the Original

Lugosi may have been the first and best Dracula, but he was far from the last. Since 1931 scores of films have featured the bloodthirsty count. True to Stoker's book in various degrees, these movies have kept the Dracula mystique alive.

Universal Studios, which released the original *Dracula*, was responsible for several of these films. Universal's efforts included two *Dracula* sequels: *Dracula's Daughter* (1936) and *Son of Dracula* (1943). The studio also released three other movies starring the head vampire himself. These films had little to do with Stoker's plot. They did, however, keep the character of Dracula in the public eye.

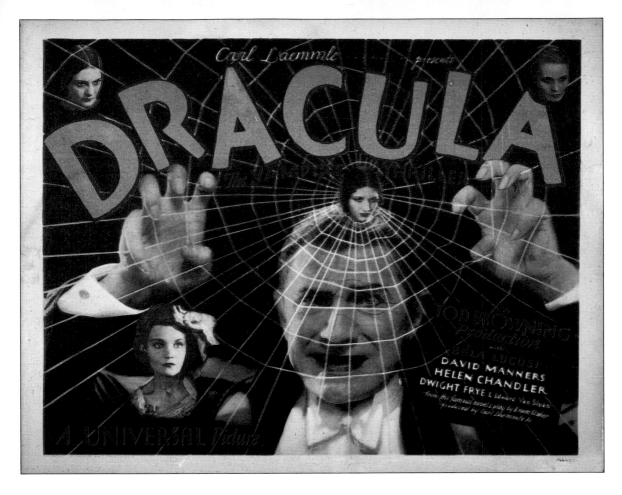

A company called Hammer Films continued this trend in the 1960s and 1970s. Hammer released eight vampire films during this period. All of the films starred Dracula and included many elements from Stoker's novel. Like Universal's offerings, the Hammer films fed moviegoers' endless appetite for all things vampire.

What they did *not* do was attempt to re-create Stoker's story line. Post-*Dracula* movies put Stoker's familiar characters into new situations. As the decades wore on and writers' imaginations wore out, the plots of Hammer's films became more and more outrageous.

In 1992 director Francis Ford Coppola decided to fix this

When the film Dracula *came out in 1931, few people had ever seen a scarier movie. Actor Bela Lugosi gave Count Dracula just the right mix of charm and menace to create an utterly frightening character.*

problem. He hired famous actors and raised $40 million to produce another film version of *Dracula*. In terms of plot, Coppola's work stuck closely to Stoker's novel. But the director upped the stakes considerably by adding big-budget elements to the mix. The result was a truly terrifying movie that featured lush sets, realistic makeup effects, a chilling soundtrack, fountains of computer-generated blood, and much more. Coppola's *Dracula* scared moviegoers silly. It also introduced a new generation of fans to Stoker's literary masterpiece.

Big Books, Big Films

Dracula is probably the vampire victor when it comes to quantity of film appearances. But Dracula has plenty of bloodthirsty company. Many other works of vampire literature have made it onto the big screen.

Richard Matheson's *I Am Legend* is one of these works. Matheson's novel was released in theaters as *The Last Man on Earth* (1964) and again as *The Omega Man* (1971). In 2007 the book was remade a third time, with its original title. The modern *I Am Legend* stars Will Smith as virologist Robert Neville. The film's daytime scenes feature striking images of a deserted, decaying New York City. The nighttime scenes are an explosion of blood-crazed, mutant vampires. With these ingredients, it is no surprise that the third *I Am Legend* was a box-office success.

Whitley Strieber's *The Hunger* also made a mark among moviegoers. The film version of Strieber's novel was released in 1983. It received poor reviews but still has managed to become a classic among vampire lovers. This success is partly due to the film's casting—Catherine Deneuve is an icily convincing Miriam, and David Bowie and Susan Sarandon are

The Other Count

Although Bela Lugosi is famous for his 1931 portrayal of Dracula, he is not the only actor associated with the role. Christopher Lee is also well known for his turn as Stoker's famous vampire. Lee starred in seven of Hammer's eight Dracula films. In doing so, he created one of the most recognizable characters in horror-movie history.

One reviewer uses these words to describe Lee's impact: "His flat demonic stare seems to ooze pure evil. . . . I challenge anybody to look Lee in the eye when he's on the hunt and not feel a frisson [shudder] of cold terror. . . . The vampire is traditionally a great evil force of destruction [and] Lee never lets you forget it."

There is no question that Lee helped to define the role of Dracula. The actor has not, however, let the role define *him*. Lee, who is still working today, has appeared in over 200 vampire-free films and TV shows. But this remarkable resume has not erased the memory of Lee's vicious vampire. To many horror buffs, Christopher Lee was and still is the face of Bram Stoker's Dracula.

Willie Meikle, "Bloody Good Fun," review of *Horror of Dracula*, Amazon, April 25, 2003. www.amazon.com.

Francis Ford Coppola's multi-million-dollar film Dracula *featured lush sets, realistic makeup, a chilling soundtrack, and lots of blood. The 1992 film also introduced a new generation of fans to Bram Stoker's classic vampire story.*

perfect as the vampire's victims/lovers. Viewers are also entranced by *The Hunger*'s frank eroticism. They enjoy imagining, deliciously, what it might feel like to be seduced into the vampire life.

Seduction is also a theme in *Interview with the Vampire* (1994), the big-screen adaptation of Anne Rice's best-selling novel. The vampire Lestat has a very intense bond with his protégé Louis. Many viewers find this relationship exciting, especially since the characters in question are played by hunky actors Tom Cruise and Brad Pitt. Thanks partly to this winning equation, *Interview with the Vampire* was a worldwide hit. Today it is considered an important part of the vampire canon.

Vamping Up the Small Screen

Must-see vampire fare is not confined to movie theaters. Many popular vampire works have made it onto the small screen, too.

'Salem's Lot was one of the first books to make this leap. In 1979 King's novel was made into a four-hour TV miniseries that featured chilling special effects and plenty of vampire gore. The series also introduced one of the most gruesome

Looking Like
a Vampire

Girls and women of all ages swoon over Robert Pattinson, the actor who plays Edward Cullen in the Twilight movies. These fans might be surprised to learn that Pattinson almost lost the role because of his looks. Studio executives worried that the scruffy young actor might not be attractive enough to do justice to Edward's character.

Director Catherine Hardwicke remembers the moment the studio raised this issue. "Catherine, do you think you can make this guy look good?" executives said when she proposed Pattinson for the role.

"Here's what I'm going to do," Hardwicke responded. "I'm going to get his hair back to a different color, do a different style. He [will] work with a trainer from now on. My cinematographer is great with lighting. He will study [Pattinson's] cheekbones, and I promise you, we'll make the guy look good."

Hardwicke certainly proved herself right. Since *Twilight*'s release, Pattinson has become an international sex symbol. He has appeared on several Sexiest Man Alive lists and countless magazine covers, and he elicits hysterical screams from female fans whenever he appears in person. Apparently he looks good enough.

Quoted in Evgenia Peretz, "*Twilight*'s Hot Gleaming," *Vanity Fair*, December 2009. www.vanityfair.com

vampires ever to appear on *any* screen, big or small. In a 1979 interview, producer Richard Korbitz talked about the show's lead vampire character. "We went with the concept of a really unattractive, horrible-looking Barlow. . . . He is the essence of evil, and not anything romantic or smarmy. . . . I just didn't think it would work,"[42] he said.

Korbitz made a good choice. His Barlow *did* work—and so did the other elements of the miniseries. *'Salem's Lot* terrified viewers in a way that few other productions have ever managed. "It gave me nightmares for years,"[43] recalls one now-grown man who watched the series when he was 11 years old.

Today's teens may never see *'Salem's Lot*. But they are finding plenty of new sources for nightmares. One of these sources is *The Vampire Diaries*, a show that premiered in the United States in October 2009. Based on L.J. Smith's book series of the same name, *The Vampire Diaries* has been a hit, especially among teens. It has been well received by most critics, too. "The supernatural drama is a first-class production, featuring an insanely gorgeous cast, sharp scripts and a brooding vibe that is hard for even the most levelheaded adult to resist,"[44] raved one reviewer after watching the show's opening episode.

A small-screen vampire series with an edgier style is *True Blood*, based on Charlaine Harris's Sookie Stackhouse novels. *True Blood* airs on a subscription channel, which means it does not depend on advertiser support. The show therefore can—and does—feature disturbing themes, plots, and images that would not be allowed on network TV. This gritty approach has been very popular among vampire fans. Millions of viewers tune in each week to watch the latest installment.

Strange as It Sounds...

Anne Rice was very unhappy when Tom Cruise and Brad Pitt were chosen to play Lestat and Louis. She felt the actors did not match her mental image of the characters.

A Risky Transition

The runaway success of *True Blood*, *Twilight*, and other offerings proves that vampires make good viewing material. Indeed, vampire literature has spawned so many TV and movie hits that it might seem like a sure thing. Just put a vampire book on the large or small screen, and the screaming fans will appear.

But this is not the case. Plenty of popular vampire novels have fizzled on film. One high-profile example is *Queen of the Damned* (2002), the sequel to *Interview with the Vampire*. Starring singer Aaliyah and actor Stuart Townsend, this movie was expected to repeat *Interview*'s box-office success. Instead, it was a flop. The film barely earned back its budget despite big-name stars and a hefty marketing push.

A couple of ambitious TV shows have met a similar fate. *Dracula: The Series* (1990–1991), for example, tried to turn Bram Stoker's *Dracula* into a weekly drama. The show never really caught on with fans, and it was canceled after one season.

This was also the case with *Blood Ties* (2007–2008), a TV series based on Tanya Huff's popular Blood series. Like Huff's books, the TV series was an imaginative mix of vampire lore, romance, and detective work. This formula had impressed legions of readers, but it failed to attract viewers. *Blood Ties* ran for just 22 episodes before it was canceled.

Bringing the Undead to Life

These examples show that vampires do not have supernatural powers over the viewing public. Although vampire-themed shows and films attract attention, they do not keep it unless they are skillfully executed. Like all stories, vampire tales require good characters, plots, dialogue, acting, and scenery if they wish to maintain viewers' interest.

Strange as It Sounds...

The first script of the *Twilight* film was very different from the book. Bella was a track star, and FBI agents used Jet Skis to chase evil vampires. These ideas were eventually dumped in favor of a more faithful approach.

Assembling these elements is hard enough. But vampire material presents an additional challenge. Vampire characters have nonhuman traits, behaviors, and abilities. They might not even appear human. Filmmakers and TV directors must decide how to portray all of these things. Will the vampire's eyes glow in the dark? What shade is the creature's skin? What does it look like when the fangs grow? These decisions and hundreds of others create a movie monster. The result must match, more or less, the mental image readers have formed. If it does not, fans of a book may lose interest in a film or TV adaptation. "The book is better . . . Brad Pitt is way too pale,"[45] sniffs one person in regard to *Interview with the Vampire*.

This viewer offers a very specific criticism. Other vampire fans, however, take a broader view. They may enjoy a vampire film, but they believe the book is always better. As one avid reader puts it:

> When you read, you're creating your own movie in a sense, and [you] decide the most important parts: how the characters speak, what they look like, and what their surroundings are like. Directors don't always get it the way you would want it. . . . No film, unless you make it yourself, can truly satisfy.[46]

For this person and many others, the true vampire experience comes from the printed word. Films and TV shows may be fun, but they simply are not the real thing. This feeling has been bringing the undead to literary life for nearly two centuries. It will undoubtedly continue to do so for many years yet to come.

Source Notes

Introduction: Immortal Attraction

1. Bram Stoker, *Dracula*, 1897. Project Gutenberg, 1995. www.gutenberg.org.

Chapter 1: Laying the Foundation

2. John William Polidori, *The Vampyre: A Tale*, 1819. Project Gutenberg, 2004. www.gutenberg.org.
3. Thomas Preskett Prest, *Varney the Vampire, or the Feast of Blood*, 1845–1847. Project Gutenberg, 2005. www.gutenberg.org.
4. Prest, *Varney the Vampire, or the Feast of Blood*.
5. J. Sheridan Le Fanu, *Carmilla*, 1872. Project Gutenberg, 2003. www.gutenberg.org.
6. Le Fanu, *Carmilla*.
7. Stoker, *Dracula*.

Chapter 2: Toward the Modern Age

8. Quoted in Leonard Wolf, ed., *Blood Thirst: 100 Years of Vampire Fiction*. New York: Oxford University Press, 1997, p. 99.
9. Quoted in Wolf, *Blood Thirst*, p. 284.
10. Richard Matheson, *I Am Legend*. New York: Orb, 1995, p. 170.
11. Quoted in Craig Hamrick, "A Conversation with Dan Ross," Dark Shadows Online, 1990. www.darkshadowsonline.com.
12. Quoted in Hamrick, "A Conversation with Dan Ross."
13. Stephen King, "'Salem's Lot Inspiration," StephenKing.com. www.stephenking.com.
14. Quoted in Helen Knode, "Anne Rice: Sex, Salvation and the End of the Century," *LA Weekly*, November 30–December 6, 1990, p. 19.
15. Sebastian, "Mr. Strieber, This Sucked," review of *The Hunger*, Amazon, April 19, 2006. www.amazon.com.
16. Jessica Levai, "One of a Few Vampire Books That Really Scared Me," review of *The Hunger*, Amazon, November 24, 2004. www.amazon.com.
17. Quoted in Staci Layne Wilson, "Chelsea Quinn Yarbro: Exclusive Interview," Horror, July 13, 2006. www.horror.com.
18. Quoted in Chelsea Quinn Yarbro, "The Stealth Interview," Fall 2000. www.ChelseaQuinnYarbro.net.

Chapter 3: A Vampire for Every Taste

19. Plaque, "I Hope You Dance," review of *Dark Dance*, Amazon, August 21, 2003. www.amazon.com.
20. Christopher Gwyn, "Good B-Movie Material," review of *They Hunger*, Amazon, October 22, 2007. www.amazon.com.
21. Software Guy, "Not Your Grandfather's Vampire Story," review of *Fangland*, Amazon, July 20, 2007. www.amazon.com.
22. Software Guy, "Not Your Grandfather's Vampire Story."
23. Quoted in Belinda Luscombe, "Well, Hello, Suckers," *Time*, February 19, 2006. www.time.com.
24. Nancy Gideon, *Midnight Enchantment*. Canon City, CO: ImaJinn, 1999, back cover.
25. J.L. Evers, "A Lot of Fun," review of *Undead and Unwed*, Amazon, March 10, 2007. www.amazon.com.
26. Kevin L. Nenstiel, "That Rare Thing in Vampire Fiction: A New Idea," review of *Way of the Wolf* (The Vampire Earth, book 1), Amazon, November 16, 2003. www.amazon.com.
27. Anonymous, "13 Bullets," *Publishers Weekly*, March 12, 2007, p. 42.
28. Lisa Lampert-Weisseg. "Why All the Vampires?" *These Days*, KPBS, November 18, 2009. www.kpbs.org.

29. Quoted in Associated Press, "Vampires, Well, Come to Life in 'True Blood,'" MSNBC, September 3, 2008. www.msnbc.msn.com.

Chapter 4: Twilight and Beyond: Vampires in Teen Literature

30. Stephenie Meyer, *New Moon*. New York: Little, Brown, 2006, p. 16.
31. Quoted in Lev Grossman, "It's Twilight in America: The Vampire Saga," *Time*, November 23, 2009. www.time.com.
32. L.J. Smith, *Secret Vampire*. New York: Simon & Schuster, 1996, pp. 114–15.
33. Quoted in Michele Lee, "Interview with Nancy A. Collins," Monster Librarian. http://monsterlibrarian.com.
34. Darren Shan, *Cirque du Freak: The Vampire's Assistant*. New York: Little, Brown, 2000, p. 10.
35. Debbie Carton, "Booklist Review of *Vampire Island*," Amazon. www.amazon.com.

Chapter 5: More than Just a Good Read

36. Marcy Gomez, "Obsessing over Twilight and Can't Wait for the DVD!" review of *Twilight* (DVD), Amazon, January 9, 2009. www.amazon.com.
37. Dazzle Me Edward506, "Re: Robert Pattinson (EDWARD)," Robert Pattinson (EDWARD) forum, Twilight Teens, November 10, 2008. www.twilight-teens.com.
38. ILurveRob, "Re: Robert Pattinson (EDWARD)," Robert Pattinson (EDWARD) forum, Twilight Teens, October 7, 2008. www.twilight-teens.com.
39. Ashley Elric, "Excellent and Entertaining Movie!" review of *Cirque du Freak: The Vampire's Assistant* (DVD), Amazon, November 8, 2009. www.amazon.com.
40. Frank W. Kerstetter, "Horror Movies of the Past," review of *Dracula* (75th Anniversary Edition), Amazon, January 4, 2007. www.amazon.com.
41. Gary F. Taylor, "One of the Finest DVD Presentations I've Ever Encountered," review of *Dracula* (75th Anniversary Edition), Amazon, November 19, 2002. www.amazon.com.
42. Richard Korbitz, "Interview," *Cinefantastique*, vol. 9, no. 2, 1979.
43. Eric, interview with the author, January 28, 2010.
44. Quoted in Karla Peterson, "It's Crazy Happy Season on Fall TV," *San Diego Union-Tribune*, October 23, 2009. www3.signonsandiego.com.
45. Nelson C., "Interview with the Vampire—Review," Melo's Sun Server. http://sun.menloschool.org.
46. Tricia Ellis-Christensen, "Why Are Books Always Better than the Movie Versions?" Wisegeek, January 26, 2010. www.wisegeek.com.

For Further Exploration

Books

Stuart A. Kallen, *Vampires*. San Diego: Reference-Point, 2008.

Barb Karg, Arjean Spaite, and Rick Sutherland, *The Everything Vampire Book*. Avon, MA: Adams Media, 2009.

Eric Nuzum, *The Dead Travel Fast: Stalking Vampires from Nosferatu to Count Chocula*. New York: Thomas Dunne, 2007.

Jay Stevenson, *The Complete Idiot's Guide to Vampires*. New York: Alpha, 2009.

Bram Stoker, *The New Annotated Dracula*. Edited by Leslie S. Klinger. New York: Norton, 2008.

Leonard Wolf, ed., *Blood Thirst: 100 Years of Vampire Fiction*. New York: Oxford University Press, 1997.

Great Teen Reads

Brian Meehl, *Suck It Up*. New York: Random House, 2008. Morning McCobb, a 16-year-old vampire, is chosen to reveal vampires' existence to humankind. It is a tough job, and this book follows every twist and turn of the ordeal.

Kimberly Pauley, *Sucks to Be Me: The All-True Confessions of Mina Hamilton, Teen Vampire (Maybe)*. Renton, WA: Wizards of the Coast, 2008. Should 16-year-old Mina stay human or become a vampire, like her parents? This is the central problem of Pauley's funny novel.

Marlene Perez, *Dead Is the New Black*. New York: Harcourt, 2008. Cheerleaders are turning into vampires! High-school junior Daisy investigates this problem in a twist-filled tale.

Douglas Rees, *Vampire High*. New York: Random House, 2003. Forced to choose between Our Lady of Perpetual Homework and Vlad Dracul Magnet School, teenager Cody Eliot makes the obvious but vampire-infested decision.

Scott Westerfield, *Peeps*. New York: Penguin, 2005. In a world where parasites cause vampirism, Cal is parasite-positive, or a PEEP. This interesting book follows Cal as he tracks down others of his kind.

Web Sites

Fan Fiction (www.fanfiction.net). This site includes hundreds of thousands of works of fan fiction, many of them on popular vampire characters.

Monster Librarian (www.monsterlibrarian.com). This site offers reviews and information on horror books of all types, along with many good articles and author interviews.

The Official Website of Stephenie Meyer (www. stepheniemeyer.com). Stay up-to-date on all things Twilight at the author's official site.

Project Gutenberg (www.gutenberg.org). This Web site offers free, full-text versions of over 100,000 classic works, including most of the older vampire novels.

The Vampire Diaries: The Official Book Site (www.vampirediaries.com). This fan site covers all aspects of L.J. Smith's series, including the books, TV shows, actors, and more.

Index